This book is dedicated to my family and friends
for always encouraging me to shine bright!

www.originalmestory.com
www.erikabusseart.com

The day I discovered what I was meant to be,
was the day I picked up a pencil
and let my imagination run free.

My pencil
drew a girl.

She was perfect,
you see?
She had curly
brown hair,
just like me.

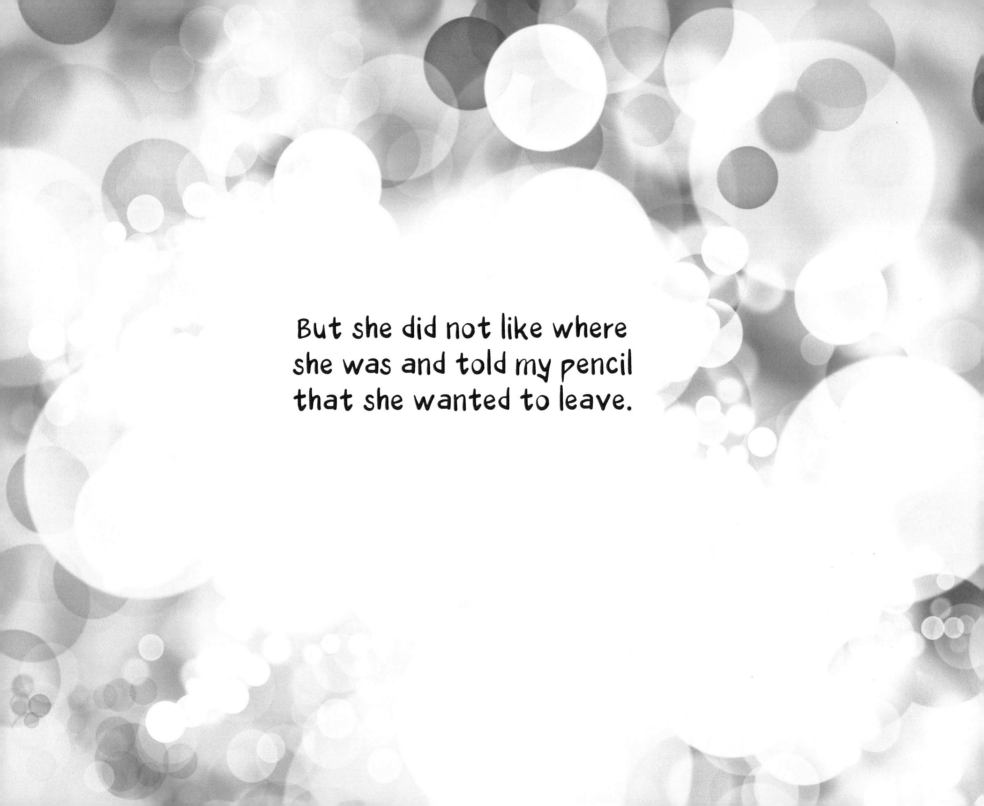

But she did not like where she was and told my pencil that she wanted to leave.

My pencil gave her a balloon,
and two and three.
She floated so high,
way up into the sky.

Past the clouds, far from the ground.

The balloons started to pop!
"Help me!" she cried.
My pencil came in to save the day,
and drew her another way.

My pencil made her a bird in a tree, that could sing any song fit for a king. She did not like this either and demanded something new - something sparkling.

My pencil made her a star, the brightest in the sky.
Her beauty was admired low and high.
But she was lonely and sad,
and wanted my pencil to make another try.

Then how about some
wacky type of machinery?

A pony?

A bowl of macaroni?

Maybe a cat?

Or a funky hat?

But none of these felt right and my pencil was starting to get uptight.

With its last power,
my pencil drew her
as a flower.

Then a tower.

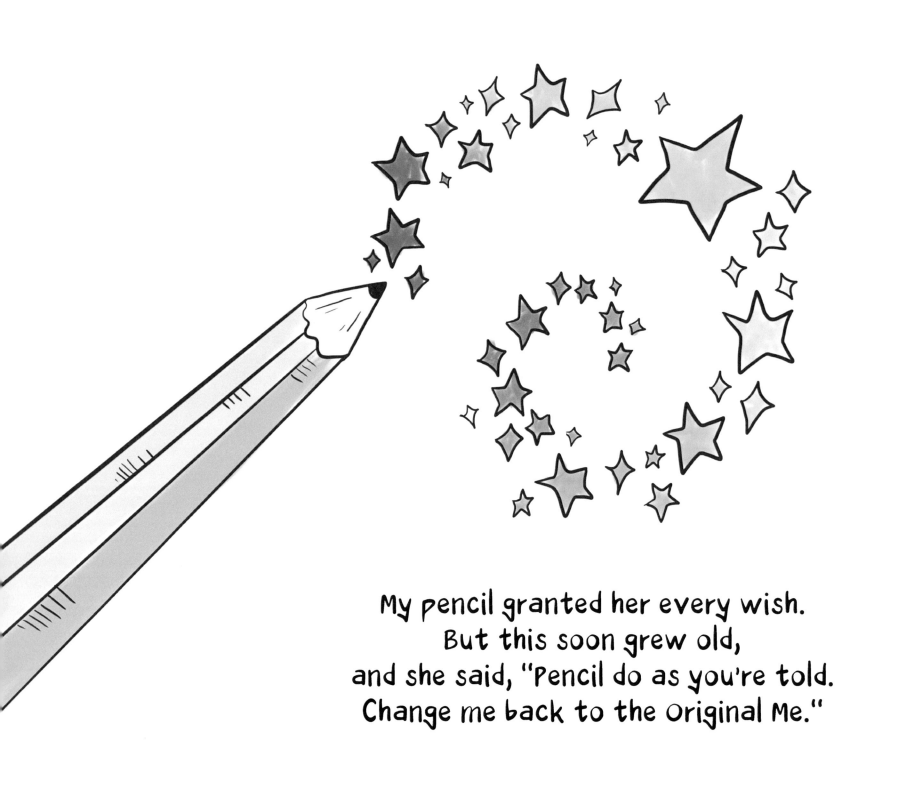

My pencil granted her every wish.
But this soon grew old,
and she said, "Pencil do as you're told.
Change me back to the Original Me."

My pencil happily drew
her back as she was.

Exactly as she was meant to be ...

Original Me!

Draw your Original Me!